To: _____

From:_____

_____

_____

_____

_____

_____

10 Traits for Enduring Ties

A Good Friend

Les and Leslie Parrott

VINE
BOOKS

SERVANT PUBLICATIONS
ANN ARBOR, MICHIGAN

Vine Books is an imprint of Servant Publications especially designed to
serve evangelical Christians.

All Scripture quotations, unless indicated, are taken from the HOLY
BIBLE, NEW INTERNATIONAL VERSION®.
© 1973, 1978, 1984 by International Bible Society. Used
by permission of Zondervan Publishing House. All rights reserved.

"Will You Be My Friend?" by James Kavanaugh is taken from his classic
book, *Will You Be My Friend?,* © 1991 James Kavanaugh and used by
permission of Steven J. Nash Publishers, publisher of all Kavanaugh's
books (800-843-8545). All rights reserved.

Published by Servant Publications
P.O. Box 8617
Ann Arbor, Michigan 48107

Cover design: D2 Designworks, Sisters, OR
Cover photograph: © Photonica. Used by permission.

98 99 00 01 10 9 8 7 6 5 4 3

Printed in the United States of America
ISBN 1-56955-058-1

LIBRARY OF CONGRESS CATALOGING-IN-PUBLICATION DATA

Parrott, Les.
A good friend : ten traits of enduring ties / Les and Leslie Parrott.
    p.   cm.
ISBN 1-56955-058-1 (alk. paper)
1. Friendship.   I. Parrott, Leslie L., 1964–   .   II. Title.
BF575.F66P37   1998
177'.62—dc21   98-14299
                                                CIP

RESOURCES BY LES AND LESLIE PARROTT

BOOKS

Relationships
Becoming Soul Mates
Like a Kiss on the Lips
The Marriage Mentor Manual
Questions Couples Ask
Saving Your Marriage Before It Starts

VIDEO CURRICULUM

Mentoring Engaged and Newlywed Couples
Saving Your Marriage Before It Starts

AUDIO PAGES

Relationships
Saving Your Marriage Before It Starts

BOOKS BY LES PARROTT III

High-Maintenance Relationships
Love's Unseen Enemy
Helping the Struggling Adolescent
7 Secrets of a Healthy Dating Relationship
Once Upon a Family

The greatest sweetener

of human life is

FRIENDSHIP.

To raise this

to the highest pitch

of enjoyment

IS A SECRET

which but few discover.

— JOSEPH ADDISON

TO

Kevin, Kathy, Rich, and Laura:

....

Good friends who raised
a European vacation
to its highest pitch
of enjoyment.

Contents

Introduction / 11

A G o o d F r i e n d ...

Makes Time / 15

Keeps a Secret / 27

Cares Deeply / 39

Provides Space / 45

Speaks the Truth / 57

Forgives Faults / 69

Remains Faithful / 77

Laughs Easily / 87

Celebrates Success / 99

Says a Prayer / 111

Epilogue / 121

Good friends. Over the years, they have comforted you, irked you and, more than a few times, saved your skin. They are the friends you have known for years but still can't wait to see next week for lunch. Loyal and lasting, these friends have stood by you in good and bad, like a pair of boots that have worn well. They are the people you wouldn't trade for anything— and if you didn't have them, you'd trade almost everything to get them. The world is a wilderness without good friends.

The young Persian soldier must have felt this acutely when he was asked by his king, Cyrus the Great, whether he would trade the horse on which he had just won a race for an entire kingdom. "Certainly not, Sire," the young soldier replied, "but I would gladly part with him to gain a good friend, if I could find anyone worthy of such fellowship."

Good friends *can* be hard to find. Acquaintances. Associates. Partners. Colleagues. These are found in abundance. Even a friend of the fair-weather variety is not uncommon. But the person worthy of being a good friend—the kind who makes time, keeps a secret, and forgives faults—is as scarce as lemonade in the desert.

Emerson, when asked about the qualities of a good friend, said, "I find very little written directly to the heart of this matter." We agree. During the last couple of decades, we have seen an inexhaustible supply of studies on marriage and family relationships. Yet the relationship between two good friends has hardly been touched. A recent study at the University of Hartford looked at scores of articles in a sample of many popular magazines and found fourteen articles on marriage and family relationships for every one article on friendship. "Our culture is obsessed with romance," the researchers concluded. "Friendship is seen as secondary; no one thinks it has to be talked about."

We've tried to change that. Every autumn on our university campus, we teach a unique course dedicated to building better relationships—especially with friends. We begin by posing a simple question to more than two hundred students: *What makes a good friend?*

Over the years we have seen responses to this question from hundreds of students, plus thousands of seminar participants. And the results have become almost predictable. In fact, the book you hold in your hands is a summary of the top ten traits people say are the most important for being a good friend. Time and again, the issues of dedication, confidentiality, loyalty, forgiveness, laughter, and all the rest vie for places at the top of the list. Each chapter of this book is our attempt to write to "the heart of this matter" by amplifying these qualities and exploring how we can make them a part of the friendships that matter most.

Les and Leslie Parrott
Center for Relationship Development
Seattle Pacific University

A Good Friend
Makes Time

> Friendship is a pretty
> full-time occupation.

TRUMAN CAPOTE

It was 9:00 on a Thursday evening and the second leg of my flight from Seattle to Colorado Springs had been canceled. I was stuck in the Denver airport and wondering how I would make it to my speaking engagement late that night at the Glen Eyrie conference center. I couldn't get through to the conference coordinators by phone, so I called a friend who lived nearby: "Barb, you won't believe where I am...." Two minutes later, she and her husband were on their way to pick me up.

My friend Lucy would have done the same thing. On more than one occasion she has whisked through our front door, arms loaded down with bags of gourmet groceries. "I'm not going to stay," she will say, "I just want to drop off a few things for your dinner tonight." Whether I'm sick or simply tired, she seems to have a sixth sense when it comes to helping out at just the right time.

So does Monty. We had just finished speaking to a group of students at a retreat center in Kentucky when we returned to our room and heard a loud knock at our door. "Monty Lobb?!" Leslie exclaimed. We couldn't believe it. Monty had driven four hours—one way—from Cincinnati and tracked us down without directions or an address. "I knew I could find you," he said with a big bear hug. "I heard you were near Wilmore and I just had to see you."

A friend to all

is a friend

to none.

ENGLISH PROVERB

We talked and laughed for about an hour and a half, then Monty had to drive home, another four hours on the road. He was teaching Sunday school the next morning at his church back in Cincinnati.

Few actions speak more loudly about the value of a good friend than making time. After all, friendships today are in a cancerous state—undernourished, withering, dying—because few people are taking the time required to keep them alive. Friends forget to phone, fail to write, ignore important events, stand each other up, and let each other down. Some try to gloss over the cause of the failure of an ill-fated friendship by saying nothing could be done to save it. They blame its demise on busy schedules, pressing deadlines, or geographical distance. But we all know that most failing friendships suffer from only one ailment: neglect.

It's no wonder that "making time" ranks high on the list of what matters most in a good friend. So many of us juggle so many things, it's easy for friendship to take a back seat. But here's news that will encourage you to put friends back at the top of your priority list. A growing body of recent research says ignoring friendship not only diminishes your quality of life but could also be a health hazard. Close friendships act as an ounce of prevention, bolstering the immune system and reducing the risk of illnesses like colds, flu, and perhaps even heart disease and other serious disorders. That makes maintaining friendships a health must, right up there with exercising and eating right.

In a landmark study at the University of Michigan, researchers analyzed all the relevant evidence they could find and discovered that people with strong ties to family and friends had a significantly longer average life span than

Often we have no time
for our friends
but all the time
in the world
for our enemies.

LEON URIS

those who did not. The researchers reached the startling conclusion that the lack of supportive relationships is a factor that is as dangerous as well-known risks such as smoking, high blood pressure, or obesity.

Quite simply, research is saying that you *need* to do what you *want* to do: Make time for friends. And never let yourself feel guilty about it. We too often equate spending time with our friends as frivolous, a sign of being lazy. That's nonsense. Making time is a noble calling for kindred spirits. It refers to the ability of two people to influence and shape each other's lives by changing plans, thoughts, actions, and emotions. Making time means getting off work early to accompany a friend to an anxiety-provoking doctor's appointment. It means canceling another commitment in order to attend a friend's recital.

Six hours after Sarah's baby was born, her

God gives us our
relatives—thank God
we can choose our friends.

ETHEL WATTS MUMFORD

doctor gave her a pass to leave the hospital so she could serve as matron of honor at her friend Jean's wedding. "I showed up ten minutes before the ceremony and she was so surprised she cried and cried. Afterward Jean and her husband stopped by the hospital, still in their formal wedding wear, so they could see the baby before they left on their honeymoon." Good friends make time for each other.

We all know that good friends make time in significant life events or moments of crisis— when a friend's emotional bottoming out, for example, means canceling another commitment to provide a shoulder of support. After all, that's what friends are for. But making time in the midst of the mundane is of equal value. For some, it may require slotting time in the midst of a hectic schedule. Others may need more spontaneity. Whatever the schedule, making time is what keeps a good friendship from foundering.

Martha Snyder was a sculptor living on a low income. Ellen Weaver worked as a packager at a granola factory. The two—both around forty and living in Eugene, Oregon—used to joke that they were in their prime earning years. "That's okay," Snyder remembers saying. "We can be 'bag ladies' together when we're old. You and your cart, and me with mine." The idea stuck. Twelve years later, Bag Ladies of the World has a dozen members and has spawned four other women's support groups in Eugene and several more elsewhere. They meet once a month just to maintain their friendships. "It gives us stability and a deep-rooted connectedness," says Martha.

Remember when we were kids? The hours spent with friends were too numerous to count. But contemporary life as adults, with its tight schedules and crowded appointment books, has forced most friendships into something requiring a good deal of intentionality and pursuit just to keep it going. Let's be honest. Making time for friends means *sacrifice*. But this sacrifice is the only thing that will counterattack the urgency of life and create a space for one of the things that matters most in this life: friends.

A gossip betrays
a confidence,
but a trustworthy man
keeps a secret.

PROVERBS 11:13

A Good Friend

Keeps a Secret

It is more shameful to
distrust one's friends
than to be deceived by them.

FRANÇOIS, DUC DE LA ROCHEFOUCAULD

In a Jewish publication, I recently saw an advertisement dominated by a drawing of a very stern-looking, bearded rabbi of the nineteenth century, the Chofetz Chaim, who wrote a book about gossip called *Guard Your Tongue*. At the bottom of the page was a "hotline" number to call anonymously if you have information about a friend's potential marriage, business partner, or whatever. A rabbi at the other end will tell you whether your gossip is important enough to pass along. If not, you are counseled to guard your tongue.

Interesting, isn't it? The advertisement reveals as much about the state of our friendships as it does about our propensity for gossip. Who among us hasn't been hurt by a broken confidence? It usually begins when your friend says to you: "You have to promise you won't tell Brenda I told you this because she made me swear not to tell anyone...." It sounds very confidential. But then why is she telling you the secret? Your friend appears to be keeping a secret but isn't. Jesus understood this when he said, "Therefore, whatever you have spoken in the dark will be heard in the light, and what you have spoken in the ear in the inner rooms, will be proclaimed on the housetops" (Lk 12:3; NKJV).

We've all shared private and personal infor-

None are so fond of
secrets as those who do
not mean
to keep them.

CHARLES CALEB COLTON

mation with a trusted friend only to learn later that our friend has blabbed it to the world. But does this mean we can't expect a friend to keep a closed mouth? No. Not with a good friend. We need to tell our secrets. It helps us explore what's troubling us and sometimes leads to helpful feedback. Sharing our secrets lets us test the reaction to what we've been holding in our hearts. Not only that, it's a relief not to be the only person who has experienced a certain temptation or tragedy. It make us feel less alone when we unburden our soul and a friend says "me too" or "I understand." Sharing a secret with a trustworthy friend can bring us closer together and deepen our relationship.

But if we expect our secret to stay under wraps, we've got to find a friend who can guard his tongue. We need a friend we can trust. A friend who considers it a true privilege to hear what's on our mind and leave it at that. We need a human vault.

Before we can identify a trusted friend we must understand why some friends are not so predisposed to keep a confidence. There are a number of reasons. One is that some don't see the harm in revealing a little information. "I find that when I am gossiping about my friends, as well as my enemies, I am deeply conscious of performing a social duty," notes anthropologist Max Gluckman with tongue in cheek. "But when I hear they gossip about me, I am rightfully filled with righteous indignation."

The need to be "in the know"—to have the inside scoop—is another powerful reason some friends can't keep their lips sealed. After all, everyone enjoys knowing information that most people aren't privy to. So your friend feels special if she is among the privileged few who know why you are divorcing your husband or why you haven't spoken to your sister in years.

Experts who have studied gossip believe we all indulge in a little gossip from time to time because talking about others is a part of our behavioral makeup, ingrained in us both socially and psychologically. "If a group of friends are engaged in a gabfest, you naturally want to join in," says Dr. Jack Levin, a sociology professor at Northeastern University and author of *Gossip: The Inside Scoop.* It's that need to feel accepted that encourages the gossip at times to embellish stories about people. If he is included in the conversation, he knows he is being accepted by the group. And to be included in the conversation he has to have something interesting to say. In a university experiment conducted by Professor Levin, gossip about a campus wedding was spread among the student body of a large university. The wedding was fictitious, it never happened, yet 12 percent of the students questioned said they had attended the

Gossip

separates

close friends.

PROVERBS 16:28

wedding. Some of them even went so far as to describe the wedding gown.

There are countless reasons beyond ignorance and social acceptance that a friend might blab your secret. But whatever the cause, there is no disputing the fact that it always causes pain. Rumors travel like the wind, intensifying as they circulate. Cheap prattle, particularly that preceded by "don't tell a soul," takes on a life of its own, disintegrating in moments a friendship that has taken years to build. That's why a good friend keeps a secret. Oh, the comfort of feeling safe with a friend, having neither to edit thoughts nor weigh words. We all want that kind of a friend, but we do well to remember that we must also be that kind of friend.

For most of her life, Kathie Lee Gifford has followed the same morning ritual. Before breakfast, before her feet even touch the floor, she says a prayer: "Lord, please help me today.

Don't let me hurt anyone with my mouth."
She writes about it in her autobiography,
I Can't Believe I Said That! I wonder if the
apostle Paul said the same thing. He certainly
warned about the condemnation that comes to
"gossips and busybodies" who say "things they
ought not to" (1 Tm 5:13). Truth is, we've all
been victims of a friend's loose lips. And we've
all hurt friends by not keeping quiet. That's
why a good friend also forgives faults.

Neither a friend nor ourselves can "unspeak"
a rumor, any more than we can snatch back a
bullet we have just fired. Once out, it is gone.
But ultimately, there is one in whom we can
always find safety, one who is supremely trustworthy. Even though we may not always
understand God's ways, we can share our
deepest secrets with him in full confidence.
David wrote about it in Psalm 62: "Find rest,
O my soul, in God alone; my hope comes from

him. He alone is my rock and my salvation; he is my fortress, I will not be shaken.... Trust in him at all times, O people; pour out your hearts to him, for God is our refuge."

Loneliness and the feeling
of being uncared for
and unwanted
are the greatest poverty.

MOTHER TERESA OF **CALCUTTA**

You're blessed when you care. At the moment of being "care-full," you find yourselves cared for.

MATTHEW 5:7 (THE MESSAGE)

A Good Friend
Cares Deeply

> To the query,
> "What is a friend?"
> his reply was
> "A single soul
> dwelling in two bodies."

ARISTOTLE

Tina came to my office on a crisp autumn morning, steaming latte in hand, and slunk into a cozy chair in the corner. We had been meeting together for four or five weeks of relationship counseling when we started exploring the issue of friendship. Tina told me she had a relational loose end with a friend she'd known since grade school. Turns out they hadn't spoken in more than a year but Tina didn't know why.

"Was there some kind of betrayal or rift?" I asked.

"Not really," Tina replied. "At least not that I can remember."

"Well then, what was it?"

Tina thought for a moment, shrugged her shoulders, then confessed: "I guess I just stopped caring."

Enough said. Once you remove care from friendship, it's over. There's nothing left to discuss. It's like removing blood from the body. Friendship cannot survive without care.

Care is so germane, so essential to the relationship that it often goes unnoticed. Ask people what matters most in a good friend and care may not make the list. But when you put this quality on a list of traits and ask people to rate its importance, you'll see it rise near the top.

Goodness consists not in
the outward things we do
but in the inward things
we are.

EDWIN HUBBEL CHAPIN

Why? Because without care friendship is impossible. Three little words—"I don't care" —are like a deadly bullet in the heart of friendship.

Frank Reed may understand the value of caring as well as anyone I know of. From 1986 to 1990, he was held hostage in a Lebanese jail cell. He was blindfolded for months at a time, living in complete darkness. He was chained to a wall and kept in absolute silence. On one occasion Reed was moved to another cell and, although blindfolded, he could sense others in the room. Only weeks later did he learn he was chained next to fellow American hostages Terry Anderson and Tom Sutherland.

In his years as a prisoner, Reed was humiliated, beaten, made ill, and tormented. But it was none of these horrific conditions that pained Reed the most as a hostage. It was the intolerable lack of concern by his captors. It was not knowing if anyone cared. In an interview with *Time,* Reed said, "Nothing I did mattered to anyone. I began to realize how withering it is to exist with not a single expression of caring around [me]. I learned one over-riding fact: caring is a powerful force. If no one cares, you are truly alone."

It seems funny that we toss this vital force around so (forgive me) carelessly. "Take care," we say to the grocery clerk who rings up our items. "Take care," we say at the end of a phone conversation with a near stranger. But when was the last time you took time to con-sider what "taking care" really means?

The word *care* comes from the Germanic *karō,* which originally meant "sad." It alludes to the idea that a caring person feels sad when you feel sad. In other words, care is a kind of com-passion that allows a friend to enter your world and feel your pain. Care says that whatever happens to you happens to me. When sadness hits you it hits me too. Of course, care also says that when something terrific happens to you, I rejoice myself. Your life makes a genuine difference to my own life. That's the essence of caring deeply.

When we truly care for a friend—at a deep and meaningful level—we involve both our heart and our head. We think our friend's thoughts and feel our friend's emotions. When we care for a friend, we pay close attention to her experience. We listen and watch for ways to be helpful. We take notice and attend to her world as if it were our own. It's what Aristotle was getting at when he said a friend is "a single soul dwelling in two bodies."

You don't have to be a hostage to appreciate the powerful force of care. All of us practice caring instinctively. Like handling a costly crystal vase, we're careful with things we value. But a good friend cultivates care at a deep level, never taking it for granted.

A Good Friend
Provides Space

> By myself I am not large
> enough to call the whole
> person into activity; I want
> other lights than my own to
> show all his facets. Hence
> true friendship is the least
> jealous of loves.

C.S. LEWIS

Jeff was one of my best friends in college—for about six weeks. We met at a student orientation meeting. All afternoon we listened to talks about campus protocol, study tips, and proper procedures. That night at dinner we ended up

I don't like to talk much
with people who always
agree with me.
It is amusing to
coquette with an echo
for a little while,
but one soon tires of it.

THOMAS CARLYLE

together in the dining hall. I was passing on the traditional hot meal choices and headed straight to the cereal bar for a heaping bowl of corn flakes. That's when I noticed Jeff right on my heels.

"You like cereal for dinner, too?" Jeff asked.

"Not really, I'm not that hungry tonight."

"I can't believe you like corn flakes with a banana on it," Jeff exclaimed. "That's exactly what I like."

As we placed our twin trays on the same table and sat down to eat, I was amazed by all the things we readily had in common. It turned out that all the classes I was enrolled in, Jeff was signed up to take as well. We lived on different floors of the same residence hall, but he was petitioning to move to the very same floor I was on. He planned to work out in the gym during the same time of day as I. It was uncanny. The list went on and on. We shopped at the same stores for our clothes. We both liked mint chip ice cream. I'd never met anyone with whom I had more in common.

As the days rolled by, Jeff and I were developing a close and comfortable friendship. It seemed almost effortless. We talked freely and frequently. Never had a cross word, or a differing opinion for that matter. We ate our meals together. Studied at the library. Hung out on the weekends. We were close—and that was the problem.

My fast friendship with Jeff eventually made me feel uneasy. Jeff, I learned, wasn't scheduled to be in the same classes as I until he discovered what classes I was taking. He hadn't planned to move to the same floor as I until he learned where I was living. Jeff probably didn't even like corn flakes. Our pseudo sameness revealed itself after a strange encounter in the campus dining hall. On this particular night I decided to eat dinner with some guys from my floor. Halfway through our meal, Jeff showed up in a huff.

"Thanks for waiting for me," Jeff sneered as he passed our table.

"What's that about?" asked one of the guys at the table.

"You got me," I said with genuine confusion.

I didn't give it more than a moment's thought until later that evening when I encountered Jeff at the library.

"You could at least say you're sorry," Jeff said before I uttered a word.

"I don't know what you're talking about," I responded.

Jeff proceeded to tell me that I was insensitive because I went to dinner without him. What's more, he told me that the date I had scheduled with my girlfriend that weekend was "uncool" because he thought we were going to the basketball game together. It was around this time that I began noticing he was drilling me with questions about anything and everything. "Who was that on the phone?" "What time do you think you'll be home from your date?" "Are you going to study with me tonight?" I started to wonder whether Jeff had become my mother inside the skin of a freshman college student. I half expected him to ask me what I was going to be wearing the next day so our clothes would coordinate.

My friendship with Jeff faded as quickly as it began. We were off to a pretty good start, I thought, but being smothered by another gets old fast. It's true of quick friends as well as those who have a long history. No matter how close the connection, there are times when we all need room to breathe. I suppose that's why so many people say a good friend provides space.

I cannot give you

the formula

for success,

but I can give you

the formula

for failure:

Try to please everybody.

HERBERT BAYARD SWOPE

There is no conversation

more boring than the one

where everybody agrees.

MICHEL DE MONTAIGNE

Without space, our relationships wither—the consuming friend leaves us gasping for air, longing for a fresh breeze.

Overly engaged and emotionally needy friends who don't know the meaning of giving another space are like a relentless heat wave. The warmth feels nice at first, but it eventually wears you down, depleting you of energy. Such friends mother and smother us with their very presence. Their constant connecting becomes oppressive—if not possessive. This kind of friend has no appreciation for what C.S. Lewis meant when he said: "In each of my friends there is something that only some other friend can fully bring out." In other words, Lewis recognized the need for space between friends. He saw the need for multifaceted relationships that help us shine where another friend, even a close one, simply is not able. This is one of the marks of a friend who provides space. He relinquishes a possessive hold and helps us cultivate other friendships.

Another mark of the space-giving friend is a solemn respect for serenity. This kind of friend recognizes the value of a thoughtful silence and a private retreat. Such people know when to bite their tongue and they know when to let you make your own path. Philosopher and author Henry David Thoreau once said, "I never found the companion that was so companionable as solitude." Let's face it, there are times in our life when we need to be alone. Times when we need to gather our wits and allow our souls to catch up. A good friend understands this. He provides space for the companion of solitude to enter your relationship.

Of course, this same friend also knows when to return, when to break the silence and rejoin your journey. Even Thoreau, who was certainly fond of solitude, noted this lonely sentence in his journal, "It would give me such joy to know that a friend had come to see me, and yet that pleasure I seldom if ever experience" (December 23, 1851). We need space for the companion of solitude, but even more we need a good friend. After all, it is this very space and separation provided by a friend that draws us back to a full appreciation of our friendship.

A Good Friend
Speaks the Truth

If we let our friend become
cold and selfish and exacting
without a remonstrance, we
are no true friend.

HARRIET BEECHER STOWE

"Les, you sometimes drive yourself so hard, pushing and pushing on an important project," someone recently told me, "that you sometimes place the same high expectations for driving hard on those around you, whether you know it or not." Ouch. Where did that come from? Talk about a zinger. Where did this guy get off telling me about how I treat other people?

Ointment and perfume
delight the heart,
and the sweetness of
a man's friend does so
by hearty counsel.

PROVERBS 27:9 (NKJV)

Actually, he had every right to tell me what he thought. John was, and is, my friend. And he was right. I can focus in on a goal so intensely that I neglect other people's feelings in the process. We were on to a second helping of spicy chicken at our favorite Chinese restaurant when he gently lowered the boom. Truth is, John wasn't trying to berate or scold me— he was actually trying to save my neck. As a good friend, he cares about me and didn't want me to get into a sticky situation with the members of a committee I was working with.

Good friends are like that. They speak the truth. Honesty is a prerequisite to their relationship. "Genuine friendship cannot exist where one of the parties is unwilling to hear the truth," says Cicero, "and the other is equally indisposed to speak it."

As painful as the truth might be, good friends are obligated to speak it. Now, this does

Be courteous to all, but inti-
mate with few, and let those
few be well tried before you
give them your confidence.
True friendship is a plant
of slow growth, and must
undergo and withstand the
shocks of adversity
before it is entitled to
the appellation.

GEORGE WASHINGTON

not mean they have license to insult, offend, and badger. The Bible talks about speaking the truth in love. And that's the goal of an honest friend. The question is, how does a friend do this? The answer involves a lot of respect. Without respect, honesty is a lethal weapon. Perhaps that's what caused Cicero to add, "Remove respect from friendship and you have taken away the most splendid ornament it possesses."

Good friends deserve the respect of knowing the truth. They deserve to know if they are hurting someone's feelings, being too aggressive, too lazy, too anything. If a friend cannot hear the truth from another friend, the relationship suffers and so does that friend.

Some time ago I (Leslie) was counseling a twenty-something student named Lisa who came to my office in hopes of resolving a problem with a close friend. Lisa wasted no time in

You can trust a friend

who corrects you.

PROVERBS 27:6 (CEV)

telling me the problem concerned her friend's stinginess.

"Jenny is so tight, she squeaks when she walks," Lisa confessed.

"Is this a new problem?" I asked.

"Oh no, it's been going on for years, but it's really wearing thin, and I find myself wanting to avoid being with Jenny whenever money is involved."

Lisa went on to tell me how meticulous Jenny can be when trying to figure out a shared bill at a restaurant. She told me about the time it took an extra ten minutes to pay for parking at a downtown garage because she wanted to make change for splitting the bill.

"How does Jenny respond when you talk to her about being so stingy?"

"Talk to her?!" she exclaimed. "I've never brought the subject up. I don't want to hurt her feelings."

Lisa and I spent the next several minutes exploring how much she valued her relationship with Jenny. Turns out, they were "best friends." But here she was, on the brink of tossing away an eight-year friendship because she didn't want to hurt Jenny's feelings. In other words, the one friendship she cared more about than any other was about to go under because she couldn't speak the truth.

Fortunately, with a little advice and coaching, Lisa mustered up the courage to confront Jenny on this annoying habit and the problem began to slowly reverse itself. The point to be learned here, however, is that friends who do not care enough to confront may save themselves a little awkwardness in the present, but they will end up losing their friendships in the future. Good friends deserve our honesty.

Honesty, by the way, is not only expressed in words, it also means being authentic as a friend.

Do not use a hatchet to
remove a fly from your
friend's forehead.

CHINESE PROVERB

Have you ever known people who become fast friends because they have so much in common? It's amazing. Their work. Their wardrobes. Their tastes. Their backgrounds. Everything seems to be in sync. Almost overnight, the two become like twins who can finish each other's sentences. That's when the red flag should go up. Why? Because the relationship isn't real. It's a pseudofriendship with the depth of a puddle. One or both of them are so eager to have a kindred spirit that they become someone they are not just to get along. The relationship becomes what Emerson called "a mush of concession" with both parties impressing each other with how much they are alike.

True friends, the kind with depth that transcends the surface and meaning that connects the souls, aren't afraid to be honest, and they aren't afraid to be themselves. True friends follow Emerson's advice: "Better be a nettle in

the side of your friend than his echo."
Translation: Speak the truth, because if you
are afraid of making enemies you'll never have
good friends.

A Good Friend
Forgives Faults

Your friend is the person who
knows all about you,
and still likes you.

ELBERT HUBBARD

Kevin is one of my best buddies. We met our freshman year in college and have been good friends ever since. But here I was, a half a country away, talking to Kevin on the phone and asking for his forgiveness. I hadn't committed a shocking betrayal or stabbed him in the back, but I had broken a promise that was important to both of us. And it hurt—him more than me. Sure, I had my reasons. At the time, at least, I thought they were pretty good. Looking back now, some ten years later, I'm not so sure. That doesn't really matter anymore, however. Kevin and I haven't talked about my broken promise for nearly a decade. Why? Because Kevin forgave me. It wasn't a flippant or sudden contrived act of forgiveness. He did some soul-searching, I'm sure. We had our share of uneasy distance. But somewhere back there, Kevin released the pain I caused and decided to remain my friend.

What a gift! Kevin, as I said, is one of my best buddies. I'd do just about anything for him, and he'd do the same for me. We're good friends, because of forgiveness. You see, when I didn't keep my word, Kevin had every reason he needed to decide our friendship wasn't worth the effort. I'd let him down, big time. He would have been justified in calling it quits if he wanted. He could have said that's enough

Treat your friends as you do
your pictures, and place
them in their best light.

JENNIE JEROME CHURCHILL

Between friends differences
in taste or opinion are irri-
tating in direct proportion
to their triviality.

W.H. AUDEN

of Les Parrott: "I don't need to waste my time cultivating a relationship with someone who doesn't deserve it." But Kevin took a different route. Instead, he set his grievance aside and granted my wish. He forgave my failing.

Good friends do that. Their survival, in fact, depends on it. Every friend we'll ever have will eventually disappoint us. We can count on it. Our friends aren't saints. They are ordinary people. Decent, yes. But even decent people hurt each other, sometimes deeply, and unfairly too. That's why a lasting friendship depends on forgiveness.

Let's get this point clear right away: Every offense of a friend does not require forgiveness. Some slights need only be overlooked and forgotten. Too many good relationships fade because some snub—real or imagined—cancels it out. Some people pout, brood, or blow up if their friend is not speedy enough in returning a phone call or if they are not included in a social event. They set such high standards for the relationship that they're constantly being disappointed. They can't let little things go. Every minor lapse becomes a major offense. So they administer forgiveness like a general anesthetic until it numbs everyone to its original effect.

Trigger-happy forgiveness is not forgiveness at all. Given out too quickly, too liberally, forgiveness becomes watered down. The quirks and cranks of our friends' annoying behaviors do not deserve forgiveness. Generosity? Yes. A sense of humor? Yes. Some tolerance? Yes. But not forgiveness. No. Forgiveness is reserved for a more serious mercy. Not for annoyances but for the deeper wrongs friends do us.

There's another important point about forgiveness: When a good friend forgives another, it doesn't guarantee reconciliation. Forgiveness requires something of the offender as well as the offended if it is to restore the relationship. My former professor Lewis Smedes is one of the nation's leading experts on forgiveness. In his best-selling book *Forgive and Forget*, he said something about what it takes to be reconciled after we forgive:

You hold out your hand
to someone who did you wrong,
and you say: "Come on back,
I want to be your friend again."
But when they take your hand
and cross over the invisible wall
that their wrong and your pain
built between you,
they need to carry something with
    them
as the price of their ticket
to your second journey together....
What must they bring?

They must bring truthfulness.

Without truthfulness, your reunion is
   humbug,

your coming together is false.

Forgiveness will always heal the wounds in our memory, regardless of how a friend responds. But reconciliation requires that our friend own up to the truth of his or her fault and see the pain it caused. No mask or manipulation is allowed. If you forgive a friend for breaking a confidence and your friend denies it ever happened, the relationship will remain in limbo. There's no way around it. Reconciliation is a two-way street, requiring both grace and repentance. And good friends know it— whether they are on the giving or receiving side of forgiveness.

A Good Friend

Remains Faithful

Will you be my friend?
There are so many reasons
why you never should.

JAMES KAVANAUGH

On August 9, 1974, after the House Judiciary
Committee had found that his actions during
the so-called "Watergate cover-up" offered suf-
ficient grounds for impeachment, Richard
Nixon resigned the office of the presidency of
the United States. And it was at his lowest ebb
in this scandal that Nixon got a letter from

Friendship is a sovereign

antidote against

all calamities.

SENECA

Harold Macmillan, the former prime minister of England. The letter read, in part, "I feel impelled, in view of our long friendship, to send you a message of sympathy and good will. I trust that these clouds may soon roll away."

Years later, when Macmillan died, Richard Nixon wrote a tribute to him in *The Times of London*. Among the things he remembered about the prime minister was his letter of friendship. "What you learn when you fail," Nixon wrote, "is who your real friends are." So true. That's why we disdain fair-weather friends who support us only when it's politically savvy, easy, or convenient to do so.

Harry Truman's secretary of state, Dean Acheson, must have understood this. He caused quite a stir when he defended his friend Alger Hiss at a press conference. Hiss was a convicted perjurer and it was bad politics to have any association with him. But when prudent politicians condemned Acheson publicly, Acheson simply said, "A friend does not forsake a friend just because he is in jail." Good friends don't desert you, even when you are in trouble. And they don't desert you when it costs them something to remain your friend. Some call this faithfulness. Others call it loyalty or consistency. Whatever you call it, however, this trait is vital to your friendships.

Think about it. Everyone, at some time or another, enters a dark day and walks as one who has the plague. Solitary. Alone. We will all experience our own private Gethsemane. And it is in this desperate time that we discover who among our friends is faithful. Those who come up empty-handed in their darkest hour may take comfort in the saying: "A dog is man's best friend." And they may be right, if no one emerges to make their road less lonely. But it is far better to travel with a companion who

The typical expression of
opening Friendship would
be something like,
"What? You too? I
thought I was the only
one"—it is then that
Friendship is born.

C.S. LEWIS

Each one helps the other,

saying to one another

"Take courage!"

ISAIAH 41:6 (NRSV)

brings the human quality of life to another proverbial saying: "A friend in need is a friend indeed." This is the mark of a good friend, that they help you out when you're in trouble.

Faithfulness is the bedrock of any committed friendship. It gives the relationship a toughness to survive. That's probably why it seems so much more horrible that Jesus was betrayed by a friend than it would have been had a stranger turned him in. So much more monstrous that Caesar was stabbed in the back by his friend Brutus than had he been stabbed by Cassius, whom Caesar did not trust anyway.

While dark days reveal and separate our fair-weather friends from the faithful, it doesn't always take a scandal or a catastrophe to bring our good friends to light. We learn which friends stick with us in the daily routine of being ourselves. We note whether or not they keep a promise. Whether they gossip behind our back. A good friend knows our heart and likes us anyway. That's the very essence of faithfulness. Tell the truth: Don't you wonder if a friend will stop liking you when you feel unlikeable? We all do. James Kavanaugh's poem cuts to the heart of our doubts:

Will you be my friend?

There are so many reasons why you never should:

Often I'm too serious, seldom predictably the same,

Sometimes cold and distant, probably I'll always change.

I bluster and brag, seek attention like a child,

I brood and pout, my anger can be wild....

And if at times I show my trembling side....

I wonder, will you be my friend?

It's a wonder any friendships survive, really. There are so many reasons each of us brings to a relationship—so many idiosyncrasies—to justify its dissolution. But that very fact is what makes faithfulness so valuable. That very fact is what has caused people down through the ages to seek a friend who sticks closer than a brother.

In the fourth century B.C., two Syracusan friends, Damon and Pythias, found themselves in a dreadful predicament. Pythias was condemned to death by the tyrant Dionysius. Knowing his friend's need to put his house in order, Damon offered to temporarily stand in place for Pythias. Dionysius agreed to the arrangement but made it clear that Damon would be killed if Pythias did not return. As promised, Pythias did return to his own execution but he met a surprise. Dionysius was so moved by the faithfulness of these two friends that he freed them both—and asked to become their friend.

A Good Friend

Laughs Easily

Laughter is not at all a bad
beginning for a friendship

OSCAR WILDE

It all started when we first met in grade school. A slight inflection. A knowing glance. Or a subtle gesture. The tiniest of things could make Greg and me laugh. We could bust up over anything and everything. And if nobody else joined in on what we thought was funny, that made us laugh all the more. On countless occasions—at church, around the dinner table, at

The greatest sweetner

of human life

is Friendship.

JOSEPH ADDISON

school—we unsuccessfully tried to swallow our laughter to prevent embarrassment. We had the same funny bone and couldn't keep from using it. No wonder we're still friends. Laughter does that. Any good friend will tell you that laughter is the shortest distance between two people.

In fact, what you find funny is a determining factor of whether or not you and another person will become and remain friends. Why? Because humor is always risky. What is appealing to some is appalling to others. In a survey of over fourteen thousand *Psychology Today* readers who rated thirty jokes, the findings were unequivocal. "Every single joke," it was reported, "had a substantial number of fans who rated it 'very funny,' while another group dismissed it as 'not at all funny.'" Apparently, our funny bones are located in different places. Some laugh uproariously at the slapstick of Larry, Moe, and Curly, while others enjoy the more cerebral humor of Woody Allen.

I'll admit that my best friends—the ones who would probably take a bullet for me—don't think twice about busting me in the chops every now and then in the name of good-natured ridicule. And it always makes me laugh. Sitting around a table at a late-night dive after a basketball game, for example, one of them might crack: "We were all impressed by that spineless prayer you call a jump shot." Which brings about the inevitable retort: "Yeah, it's about as good as that serious medical disorder you call a golf swing." Leslie thinks this is more of a "guy thing." Maybe she's right. All I know is that some best buddies would never bond without a little needless needling.

Think about Huck and Tom on the river, Butch and Sundance on the range, Hope and Crosby on the road. All of them made a friendship of mockery and became better friends

So long as we are loved by
others I should say that we
are almost indispensable;
and no man is useless
while he has a friend.

ROBERT LOUIS STEVENSON

Friendship

redoubleth

joys, and

cutteth griefs

in half.

FRANCIS BACON

because of it. Now, some people who just don't get it say this is a pathetic way to show affection. Maybe so, but try telling that to a small group of smart-aleck friends sitting inside a cozy, satiric circle.

Of course, this isn't my primary mode of connection with my good friends. Truth is, we can be as tender as we are tough. The point is that when it comes to humor, it takes all kinds. That's what makes sharing a laugh with another person so special—and so risky. Humor is a litmus test for mutual understanding between two people. Sometimes it fails miserably, but it can also reveal the possibility of a new connection. Perhaps more importantly, laughter is the fuel that keeps good friendships going once they are born. It's what enables friends to help each other cope in the midst of crisis. After all, where would we be without someone who could make us laugh?

Consider Janet, a young attorney, who wanted to impress her potential partners with an elaborate dinner. She and her friend Alison cooked all day, and then Alison, in a traditional uniform, served the meal. All went well until the main course. As Alison was bringing in the crown roast, the kitchen door hit her from behind and the platter flew across the room. Janet froze, regained her composure, then commanded, "Dear, don't just stand there. Pick up the roast, go in the kitchen, and get the *other* one!"

Eve Arden, the actress who portrayed Miss Brooks on the popular 1950s television show of the same name, dealt with a practical joke that was sprung on her the closing night of one of her stage performances. Arden's costar and friend had the sound man ring the prop telephone in the middle of her monologue at a time not specified in the script. When the phone rang, Arden picked it up, paused, and then handed it to her leading man. "It's for you," she said.

Humor helps us cope—not just with the trivial but even with the tragic. Psychoanalyst Martin Grotjahn, author of *Beyond Laughter*, notes that "to have a sense of humor is to have an understanding of human suffering." Charlie Chaplin could have said the same thing. Chaplin grew up in the poorest section of London. His mother suffered from serious mental illness, and his father died of alcoholism when Charlie was just five. Laughter was Chaplin's tool for coping with life's losses. Eating a boiled leather shoe for dinner in his classic film *Gold Rush* is more than a humorous scene. It is an act of human triumph, a monument to the coping power of humor.

One does not need to be a professional comedian, however, to benefit from comedy.

Victor Frankl is another example of how humor can empower a person to contend with horrendous circumstances. In Frankl's classic book *Man's Search for Meaning*, he speaks of using humor to survive imprisonment during World War II. Frankl and another inmate would invent at least one amusing story daily to help them cope with their horrors.

"If you can find humor in anything," according to Bill Cosby, "you can survive it." Researchers agree. Studies reveal that individuals who have a strong sense of humor—who can laugh easily with at least one other person—are less likely to experience depression and other forms of mood disturbance.

Scientists hypothesize that humor helps us cope because it offers a fresh perspective. When the naturalist William Beebe used to visit his friend President Theodore Roosevelt at Sagamore Hill, both would take an evening stroll after dinner. Then one or the other would go through a customary ritual. He would look up at the stars, saying, "That is the Spiral Galaxy of Andromeda. It is as large as our Milky Way. It is one of a hundred million galaxies. It is 750,000 light years away. It consists of one hundred billion suns, each larger than our sun." Then silence followed. Finally, one of them would say, "Now I think our problems seem small enough."

Every good friend knows that humor lends a fresh eye to our troubles and gives us a new perspective.

A Good Friend

Celebrates Success

> Most people enjoy the
> inferiority of their
> best friends.

LORD CHESTERFIELD

She came to my house every day, bearing freshly squeezed orange juice, pots of chicken soup, and loads of advice. My friend Kelly (not her real name) was a godsend, there for me at a horrible time when I was going through a tough spot at work and trying to pick up the pieces after my parents' divorce. I'd weep, and

The deepest principle

in human nature

is the craving for

appreciation.

WILLIAM JAMES

she'd put her arm around my shoulder, bucking me up and reassuring me that I would begin feeling better soon. When things didn't improve at work and I continued to wrestle with my parents' situation, she'd come over, listen to my new tale of woe, and tell me my limitless talents would soon take me out of despair.

Kelly was as solid as a friend could be—until I made a career transition and my life began looking up. Then this woman who had been on the scene in my darkest days seemed to suddenly vanish. My phone calls to her went unanswered, and when I did finally reach her, there was coldness in her voice instead of enthusiasm at my good fortune. I agonized: What had I done to drive her away? I missed her, but she didn't seem to miss me. I felt as if I had been dumped. And indeed I had. From her point of view, with my crisis over, there was no place for our friendship to go except out the window.

Certainly, a defining trait of a good friend is the ability to stick with us in bad times. No one argues that. But sometimes we discover, painfully, that the true test of a friend's staying power is her ability to be supportive when things are going well.

Kelly, it turned out, was a perfect example of a foul-weather friend, someone who thrives during your disasters but becomes scarce when things improve. This kind of friend works to ferret out your troubles and even creates some you didn't know you had. But when the troubles don't exist, neither does she. Why? Because her role as a friend—or more accurately, as a "crutch"—is threatened when circumstances change. If you aren't needy, so the reasoning goes, you may not need her. So she wants to keep you in a needy state and finds it impossible to hang around if you're not.

In each of my friends
there is something that
only some other friend
can fully bring out.

C.S. LEWIS

Man lives more by

affirmation

than by bread.

VICTOR HUGO

A good friend, on the other hand, does quite the opposite. She celebrates your success. She spreads the good news and is happy for your achievement. Of all the traits a good friend possesses, in fact, this one may be the most telling. And the most challenging. After all, almost anyone can befriend someone who is down on their luck. At some level, it makes us feel better about ourselves when we aren't the ones in anguish. By comparison, we think, we're doing pretty good. But when your best buddy hits a windfall? Gets engaged? Gets a promotion? A pay raise? Some notoriety? That can try even the most committed of friends.

So what's a good friend to do? The answer is probably not what you want to hear. It involves taking a wide-eyed look at the parts of yourself you wish didn't exist. It involves scrutinizing your jealous, suspicious, cynical, resentful, and competitive side. It means owning up to the fact that you may like serving as your friend's lifeguard more than as a cheerleader. Sure, it's an ugly side, but it's better to own up to it than allow it to keep you from being the kind of friend you want to be. In fact, if you don't come to terms with how you really feel about your friend's good fortune, you'll never be able to genuinely enjoy it. What's worse, your friend will know it.

Former therapist Carmen Renee Berry, who wrote *Girlfriends: Invisible Bonds, Enduring Ties* (Wildcat Canyon Press) with Tamara Traeder, believes celebrating a friend's success can be especially difficult for women. She says most women don't know how to manage their competitive or envious feelings with friends because we have never had a chance to learn. "We weren't raised to beat our friends in games like men were," she notes. "We always did things together, and usually the activities

106

weren't competitive. It takes a lot of courage for a woman to acknowledge her competitive feelings; but if she doesn't they will become an unconscious barrier, and they will not help the friendship."

No matter what your gender, there is always potential for an unconscious barrier to keep you from celebrating your friends' success. The temptation is to bring friends down to earth when they are flying high. And we do it in the pious name of not wanting them to get a "big head." We become the ego police and wrangle their self-esteem in order to inflate our own.

I (Les) was recently giving a series of lectures in Australia when I discovered a fascinating phenomenon I'd never heard of before. It's called the "tall-poppy syndrome." Over the years, it has become such a part of the Australian culture, so ingrained, I couldn't find anyone who could tell me its origin. But everyone knew the experience and how it worked. In Australia, if one person begins to succeed, if he grows taller than all the rest, it's up to his chums to cut him down to size. They make it a point to cheer on the underdog, never the top dog. I suppose we have the same thing in the States, to one degree or another. On my own university campus we call it egalitarianism. And no one, in the academic's ideal world, should win any special favors. Promotions are calculated and dispensed on a strict schedule once someone meets the demands of predefined criteria. Unlike the real world of business, for example, there's no wiggle room or fast track for special cases. We all must fit the same mold, or at least pretend to. But in Australia I was surprised to discover that an entire culture, not just a college campus, could be concerned with cutting down people who pull away from the pack.

I can't speak firsthand about the state of friendships in Australia, but I can tell you that anyone who practices the tall-poppy syndrome with his friend is missing out on a great deal of joy. Nothing takes the wind out of the sails of friendship more than wondering why your friend doesn't recognize your accomplishments. After all, a real friend—a good friend—not only lends a hand when you're in need, he applauds your success and cheers you on when you prosper.

A Good Friend

Says a Prayer

> God does nothing but in
> answer to prayer.

JOHN WESLEY

Albrecht Dürer wanted to paint ever since he was a child. When he was old enough, he left home to study the great art and artists of the world. Along the way, Albrecht became friends with a fellow student who shared his passion for art. As starving artists, the two beginners found it difficult to make a living and study art at the same time. That was when Albrecht's

None goes his way alone:

All that we send into

the lives of others comes

back into our own.

EDWIN MARKHAM

friend offered a tremendous sacrifice—he would work while Albrecht studied. The idea was that once Albrecht's paintings began to sell, his friend would then have his chance.

At first, Albrecht resisted his friend's offer, but after much persuasion he agreed. Albrecht worked faithfully as an artist while his friend toiled long hours to make a living.

The day came when Albrecht sold a wood-carving and his friend went back to his first love. As he began to paint once again, he made a dreadful discovery: the hard work he had done to make a living had stiffened and twisted his fingers. He could no longer paint with skill.

Albrecht was filled with deep sorrow when he learned what had happened to his friend. One day as he was returning home unexpectedly, he heard the voice of his friend praying quietly for him, with his gnarled, toilworn hands folded before him.

A friend may well be
reckoned the masterpiece
of Nature.

RALPH WALDO EMERSON

It was that image that inspired Albrecht to paint something that has since become world famous. "I can never give back to my friend the artistic skill he sacrificed for me," said Albrecht, "but I can show him how much I appreciate what he did for me by painting his hands, folded in prayer."

Albrecht Dürer's inspired painting is recognized today by millions around the world who are blessed by the image of the classic clasped hands. And friends who know the story behind the painting are doubly blessed by the message.

Prayer catapults friendship into the deepest and highest work of the human spirit. "Prayer—secret, fervent, believing prayer—lies at the root of all personal godliness," writes William Carey. To pray is to change. When we pray God slowly and graciously reveals to us our hiding places, and sets us free from them. In prayer we begin to think God's thoughts and see our relationships from God's point of view.

How does praying for a friend begin? By centering down and listening to the quiet thunder of the Lord. It begins by attuning ourselves to divine breathings. Søren Kierkegaard once observed: "A man prayed, and at first he thought that prayer was talking. But he became more and more quiet until in the end he realized that prayer is listening." Listening to God is the necessary prelude to intercession. We must hear the will of God before we pray it into the life of a friend.

In times of meditation there may come a rise in the heart, a compassionate compulsion to intercede. This inner "yes" is the divine indication to fervently pray. We are told that Jesus was "moved with compassion" for people. This compassion is one of the clearest indications that you are called to pray for your friend. After all, when you genuinely love a friend, you

116

Best friend,

my wellspring

in the wilderness!

GEORGE ELIOT

desire for them far more than it is within your power to give, and that will cause you to pray. And if you are filled with compassion for your friend you will eventually know what to pray for.

Of course, there are plenty of times when we do not *feel* like praying for a friend. When a friend is enjoying the excitement of success, we are not likely to be compelled with compassion, for example. But prayer is like any other discipline. We may not feel like practicing the piano, but once we play for a while we feel like doing it. In the same way, our prayer muscles need to be limbered up a bit, and once the blood-flow of intercession begins, we will find that we feel like praying.

You may wonder, at a practical level, what does all this talk of prayer have to do with being a good friend anyway? Here's our answer:

Prayer enables us to make time for a friend when the urgency of life is keeping us apart.

Prayer enables us to keep a confidence when we are tempted to let the secret slip.

Prayer enables us to speak the truth to a friend when it would be easier to pretend it didn't need to be said.

Prayer enables us to forgive a friend's faults by surrendering our right to hurt back just to even the scale of justice.

Prayer enables us to remain faithful to a friend, even when we could find plenty of reasons to let the friendship fade.

Prayer enables us to laugh more easily with a friend by seeing the funny side of life.

Prayer enables us to celebrate a friend's success with a genuine spirit of gladness.

The bottom line? Prayer enables us to be a good friend.

Epilogue

The Scottish philosopher David Hume, in 1740, said, "The difficulty is not so great to die for a friend, as it is to find a friend worth dying for." That's a catchy saying, but we think David Hume had it backwards. The real difficulty in finding a good friend is trying to be the kind of friend we want to find. Too often we *look* for a good friend before we work on *being* a good friend. Dale Carnegie, friendship guru and author of the mega-best-seller *How to Win Friends and Influence People*, said, "You can make more friends in two months by becoming interested in other people than you can in two years by trying to get people interested in you."

Our prayer is that you might enjoy the company of a good friend. But remember: "Greater love has no one than this, that he lay down his life for his friends" (Jn 15:13).

About
the Authors

Drs. Les and Leslie Parrott are codirectors of the Center for Relationship Development at Seattle Pacific University (SPU), a ground-breaking program dedicated to teaching the basics of good relationships. Les is a professor of clinical psychology at SPU, and Leslie is a marriage and family therapist at SPU. The Parrotts are authors of the Gold Medallion Award-winning *Saving Your Marriage Before It Starts, Becoming Soul Mates,* and *The Marriage Mentor Manual.* They have been featured in

The New York Times and *USA TODAY*, and have appeared on *The Oprah Winfrey Show*, *CNN*, *CBS This Morning*, and *NBC Nightly News with Tom Brokaw.*